Straight Razor Days

Straight
Razor Days

Joel Thomas Hynes

PEDLAR PRESS | Toronto

ACKNOWLEDGEMENTS
The publisher wishes to thank the Canada Council
for the Arts and the Ontario Arts Council for their
generous support of our publishing program.

LIBRARY AND ARCHIVES CANADA
CATALOGUING IN PUBLICATION

Hynes, Joel, 1976-
    Straight razor days / Joel Thomas Hynes

Poems.
ISBN 978-1-897141-42-7

    I. Title.

PS8615.Y54S87 2011   C811'.6
C2011-904307-6

COVER ART
Michael Pittman *Hunter (encepholopathic bear)*

DESIGN
Zab Design & Typography, Toronto

TYPEFACE
Bembo

Printed in Canada

THE CANADA COUNCIL | LE CONSEIL DES ARTS
FOR THE ARTS | DU CANADA
SINCE 1957 | DEPUIS 1957

ONTARIO ARTS COUNCIL
CONSEIL DES ARTS DE L'ONTARIO

For Jenny Rockett, lusty and lovely

And in memory of Thomas Hynes

Contents

Exit 31

Book Burnings

The Very Back Room

"Let's go," he said, "as fast as we can. No one loves us here."
— GABRIEL GARCÍA MÁRQUEZ

Exit 31

The Day On Paper

I only had to ask the boy
once this morning
to get up for school.
He marched down the stairs,
all smiles, ate his whole breakfast
pensive, without fuss,
had his uniform on
before the coffee hit my brain.
He was waiting in the porch come eight-fifteen,
and we were off.

I took in an early Meeting then,
tapped into that whole higher power business.

Because I've been hoarding those royalties
I picked up a load of pressure-treated
and rebuilt the back deck before ten oclock.
Then a priest came by,
one whom I'm quite fond of,
and anointed it with holy water
so that every barbecue hereafter
will be a roaring success
of flame-broiled ecstasy.

After that I stripped down the GS850
and figured out it was just a silly base-pan gasket
that I resealed myself to save some further bucks.
It'll never act up again.
Upon a test ride I discovered
the old girl could finally do
what the speedometer says she can do.
So I drove out to motor vehicle

and had her registered
and insured.

Next I hightailed it to the house in Scilly Cove
and tore off the worst of the clapboard,
replaced a couple of the larger windows,
patched that bastard leak around the chimney,
hauled away the last of the fence,
whipper-snipped the front yard,
culled the alders
and lugged the old collapsed stable
to the dump.

Back to St. John's to collect the boy before five.
On the way in
I stopped off for a meal at Legge's
and finally nailed that waitress with the trashy highlights.
Called my girlfriend and told her about it.
She laughed, said I was a wild one
and to please save some for her.

To the bank and settled up
that niggling mortgage.
Quick drink with the taxman.
Then the boy's supper,
all veggies and tofu, which he devoured.
Then he did the dishes
and dove in to his homework.
I tried to get him to watch some TV
but he would not,
said he had laundry to do.
He was waiting in bed
with teeth brushed and fingernails trimmed
before I even had the teabag in the cup.

He told me a bedtime story
about a writer who wins six million dollars
and collects vintage motorcycles
and never writes another word for the rest of his life.
I cried at the end.
All this by eight oclock.

Then a gracious, conscientious letter
to Ms. Hunter in Vancouver,
Dyane on Rexton Island,
Alicia in Harlem,
Jenny in Brandon,
each word deliciously placed
and damn near romantic.

To the truck for a major victory with a rear sway bar.
Every tool I needed was right there in the box.

After that my father called
to tell me
he was always jealous of my brains, that mine
were the finest books he's ever read
and that he heard I had a cock
to rival a French baguette.
I told him if it was clemency he was looking for,
then he dialed the right number.

Before lights out I wrapped up my novel.
Christ, it all came so clear in the end.

Postcard from the Land of the Living

Well you know I'll have to stick it to him, pin him down in some
insufferable public arena and force him to declare
that he was not capable of knowing me
the way
I should have been known.

And once it's out, it's out and I'll goddamn well laugh
and roll about feverishly, as if any of it mattered.

There'll be a standing ovation for one or the other,
and I'll snigger myself to sleep that very night.
Blood on my pillowcase
come morning.

He's far away now, kicked off in another time, lounging roughly
in the land of the living.
I am the furthest blunder from his heart.
The world in which I crave reprisal no longer exists.

Lookit, you can squander a lifetime waiting to be released,
hovering about the mailbox, aching
for that certain glimmer
in the postman's eye.

All Black from Here

She's away, away for the mainland. I have her key and her roommates loathe me because I gorge drunken savage late night through the fridge, roaring down the hallway, stumbling into bedrooms with that day-old sour liquor stench. I steal lotion, books, movies, spare change, leather things. I read diaries, I hoard and hide and rifle through laundry baskets looking for moist lacy underwear to cozy up with.

All the juice in the fridge is marked with greasy black marker at the level of the latest drink. Each tub of butter has a name tag hastily taped across the lid with an exclamation point at the end of each owner's name.

One night the roommates appear to be waiting up for me after a house meeting, of sorts, but I quickly turn it around on them with a moan and groan about the state of my freshly infected arm. They all gather round (one with a cloth, one with an icepack) while I slur through the horrors of the needle. How he scraped it back and forth and back and forth like a rusty scalpel because he was new to the black works and didnt know enough to simply tickle the ink in. How he wanted to add some colour, but I declined, told him I was going black from here on in.

My arm wont bend at the elbow and my shoulder seizes with an exotic pain. There's talk of the hospital, talk of calling my girlfriend on the mainland, and then someone lays me out in the wrong bed, brings me a glass of juice with vodka from a bedside cupboard I hadnt thought to pillage. There's a perfume, a softness I'm not use to, wet lips down there.

Book Burning

That's the last from the box,
thank Christ.
My hands were beginning to cramp.

On this last copy I crack the spine
then rip the whole book in half
with as much ceremony as if
it were a six-month-old phone bill.
Drop the pages into another roaring blaze,
another howling back meadow pyre
of failed clapboard
splintered fencing
shamed window frames
and half rotted tarpaper eaves:
my most satisfying creation to date.

The wind turns,
a scorching tongue licks out
to singe my hangdog scruff.
I ignore the faint stiffening
just below the drawstring of my coveralls.

A notably angry pop of sparks and ember.
One renegade page
defects into the night air,
then settles on the toe of my boot.
The top half of the page is burned away,
leaving a lone paragraph
(written some lifetime ago by my own hand).

You cant force symbolism Fucko.
Your life is a black lie
and the wash is just about ready
for folding…

Minutes, seasons pass, my eyebrows crisping,
the woods at the edge of the meadow flickering
with the vigilant eyes of creatures
that want in
on what they are outside of.

Lob another turncoat junk into the centre of the pit.
A nearing presence, a vehicle.
No one ever comes up my road.
Thick dead of a night like this.

I shoulder the spade and swagger out
to meet the lights.
Maybe a carload of buck Protestants
come to do a number
on the dirty heathen on the hill.

I'll have fun with this shovel before they take me down.

Apparently

He had that quiet air,
so they stuck him on the big gun his first week on board.
He took to it like a fiend, mowing down anything that moved:
Focke-Wulf, whitecaps, kittiwakes – no exceptions.

When it was all over he still hadnt
tempered the fever
so sailed away for forty more years
of whoring and boozing and brawling.

He was up to sixty smokes a day, them days,
and when he came home to stay
he tossed a full pack off the wharf
and never thought of them again.

When Bill H wouldnt cough up what was owed,
he flung a three hundred pound anchor down
through Bill's engine house
and called it even.

Fussy about boots,
he could talk at length
on the import of mink oil and Vaseline
and had several lively versions
of how he came to own a certain leather coat:
backroom blackjack in New Orleans
bare-knuckle rumble near Hudson's Bay
bullied off the back
of one colossal stevedore
in Old Montreal.

Shortly before his ninetieth
he woke up to find it too hot in his room
and in his one-piece long johns crouched down
and ripped the baseboard heater clean out of the wall.

He went away quietly,
so quiet they were nervous to lead him by the elbow
or speak of the world out there
or mention unfamiliar names.

I Never Dream of My Father

A banshee howls here and there,
her fevered pitch toothless in the predawn mist.
My father registers her shriek
turns luxuriously in his bunk and sinks
back down to the deepest sleep he's ever known.

I never dream of my father,
his years outspread,
unfolded, long since divvied out
to the derelict autism of the barrens.
Perpetual Long Beach roll
pounding his heart to sleep each night.

The death toll has been too conclusive
round these parts already.
She wails for the rest of the world,
that other world,
not the one he's chosen.

When she comes for him
she will come with a grace,
a mercy
set aside for hearts too frail
to ever fully walk away.

In the Very Back Room

The boy found a couple of rat skeletons huddled together
in a grubby nest of blanket fluff. He spray-painted them
chrome and set them on my windowsill to dry. From this
angle, tonight, it's difficult to decide if these rats went
peacefully or if they suffered: ghastly miserable starvation
deaths. Certain creatures possess that unnerving duplicity
even when all the flesh has rotted from their faces. Yesterday
the boy took off on a big jet plane, so I've sulked off to my
woods again. I cant imagine not drinking that dozen and
a half cans cooling in the well at the top of the meadow.
The windup transistor tells me it's raining hard in St. John's
tonight. Out here the sky is close and filled with the fiction
of fair news. I've a good fire in the pit, burning copies of
National Geographic from 1978.

Not a breath of wind. But the rain is coming. It's coming.
It'll hit hard when it does, and I'll be grateful for it.
Drown out all thought, batter and roar off the roof, the
windowpanes, and thieve me away to the easiest sleep *I've*
ever known. I'd like to believe that. But soon enough I'll
be ranting at the floorboards, snarled up in my ragged wool
blanket, thrashing through another nightmare of gargantuan,
chrome-drenched creatures hulking down from the woods
to devour the one part of me worth hunting for. And by the
time I'm found they'll not be able to discern if a scream, a
belly laugh, or a battle cry has claimed the final expression
on my face.

Dream of His Old Ford Custom

The cuffs of my pants are drenched through,
but the boots are warm and dry.
I'm arrested between the world that is
and the one that's yet to come.
Mighta been drinking with strangers again,
spewing tall tales
they have no means of discrediting.
The old road is murky, inconsolable black,
my eyes pasted to the ground
as though wary of the next foothold,
or trying to locate an item
misplaced years ago;
pale rumour of an article I've hunted
since before I learned to covet.

It's an item someone else has lost,
or deserted, or hidden from themselves,
and so carries all the counterfeit credence of the fable:
near finished journal of a man long passed,
engraved commemorative pen,
tarnished wedding brooch,
the errant head of a rusted claw hammer.
Some *thing*
with the burden of history much more dear
than the thing itself.

I've only gone and abandoned my truck.
She's slunk in the ditch by the post office,
dead in the alders behind the Orangemen's Hall,
smashed half through the porch at Jack B's summer place,
parked smartly in the gravel pit near the old dump.
She's the same monstrous shade

as this doomsday hour
and I could stagger face and eyes into her at any moment.

There's been a strong northeasterly
these past three days.
I spy a shoddy piece of clapboard
in the gutter to my left.
Scour the road for more fragments of my home,
but there is only this one piece.

My truck is parked here,
askew at the crest of the hill, defeated
like an old neglected nag.
Failing alternator, filter change.
Things that scramble my brain
like algebra, level and plumb,
ground wires, carbohydrates,
political theory
and literary structure.

Rounding the rear end of the truck
I see it's now a rust-patched grey, instead of black.
Open bed, tailgate, sawdust swirling in back.
A machine built for work, not show.
It's my father's trodden Ford Custom,
scrapped and dumped some twenty years ago.
The sight sets my blood to hurry:
more men's business I've shrunken away from.
The house my father built with his own hands
was carted home, piece by piece, in the bed of this truck.

Once, driving through LaManche Bottom
with a load of sweet cedar shingles,
the tarp's manic flapping,

my father switched off the radio
and slipped the stick to neutral,
strained his ear towards the dash
to identify the latest grumble beneath the hood.
When we stalled at the bottom of Hell Hill
he took his battered claw hammer,
popped the hood and made
a muted, tinny wallop
then climbed back inside,
turned the key
and we were off again.
Just like new, he said,
just like new.

Book Burning

The burn out there, these nights,
has settled its debts again,
smoldered off to the shadows like a difficult face
from another unsound dream.

The burn in here
swaggers on.

He heard her say
he flushed the whole bottle
down the toilet,
as quick as that, the bastard.

Nothing more to be done
but let the old devils cool. Fasten the latch.
Check the burners.
Pull the shade.
Offer the nod,
repent, repair.

He heard her say
you might as well
go back to your dope
for all the stupid books
you read.

Here, she says, *read this one.*
Swear someone followed me around
and wrote all my shit down.
Go on, she says, *you always complain*
that I dont let you in.

She flips her skirts
at a phantom cabbie,
scuffs home through the ruins,
tries to keep the best story straight.
He heard her say
I just want to see
what all the fuss is about.

He heard her say
does anyone ever think
to feed that cursed dog?
The bedside clock gave up the ghost
at a quarter to five near on three weeks ago.
There's that roofer's rig
with the haughty lettering
parked just so across the road.

Her finest nightdress
with the bakeapple smudge
and the torn hemline
draped across the bedroom door
like a spectre,
leering like old gossip.

Slow blue smog gathered
above his pillow, ashes
crushed into the margins.
He heard her say
bet you wish you'd never
cracked the spine on that one.

He heard her say
it's like this love — it's not
this way anymore.

Letter to Dermot

Been meaning to write a letter to Dermot.
You know how that goes – nothing much happens
until everything does,
and by that time
it's too late
to fit it into an envelope.

He crosses my mind
while I'm racing down Blackmarsh
with the power steering pump moaning bloody hell
and the bakery girls leaning into three oclock smokes,
and me gawking at this one
and that one,
saying to myself
No I wouldnt,
no I would not,
I would never.

It's off to the bank for the ex
and then to the landfill
for the one I'm barely holding onto.
The boy is good until five oclock
and then I will begin again,
thinking and talking and behaving another way.
He needs that.
And I look forward to the shift in me.

Down in Robin Hood Bay amidst the squalor of gulls
and the thick, punchy stench of useless urge,
she sits in the passenger seat waiting patiently to leave me
whilst I heave into the pit,
with all this bygone unchecked anger,

the cumbersome bags of dirt and leaves and dogshit.
She loves a trip to the dump,
but she never sets foot outside the truck,
only offers to help once I've got a good
momentum up.
I dont mind.
I've never needed a hand
when it comes to a violent act.

I drop her home before she can find the words,
her most assertive tone,
and then with an hour to kill
I think of Dermot.
I fret about his harvest and his health,
his famous sessions with the bottle
on the other side of the Atlantic,
his half-written epic driving Helen mad.

Sharpen my pencil and empty the ashtray.
Twist the handle of my mug to the left.
Lean in gravely over the desk.

Apparently

Straight A student
the whole way up,
never late, never kept in,
never once felt the stinging shame
of a nun's strap.

Never drank, *never* smoked,
wouldnt know the smell of weed
from offal.

Kept to himself, kept to himself.
Pliability of the middle child,
civil, appeasing, nondescript,
cradled his solitude
with a quiet pride.

Never fought: picked that one racket
with a lad from the north side.
Something to do with true love,
the first
and only.
Met her when they were each thirteen
(meaning none came before
and none came after).
Walked the road between hers and his
back and forth so often, so often,
he could stop and tie his laces
at the mouth of the graveyard
on the blackest November night.

Once, a short ways past the old Legion,
a rat the size of a small dog shot out of a drainpipe
and caught him by the ankle
and he never even flinched,
stomped it back into the gutter without so much
as a dirty word uttered.

Around the Corner
(for B. Harvey)

Sluggish weeknight, out for a romp with the dog. Summer
pending with all its muggy pledges. And here's Harvey
outside the shop on Queen's Road. Lives just around the
corner now. He's had a craving for Coke, pulls the bottle
out of the bag. Not just Coke, he says, but the old time
bottle, like the movies. He holds the leash while I go buy
one for myself. We lean against the shop front, drinking,
puffing away. It's like old times without the handcuffs. He
admits he's been listening to too much Cohen. There's some
artsy dreadlocked girl in Montreal who keeps threatening
to come visit him. Says she's got a new double bed and
that her sister was a stripper, but lately volunteers for some
church crowd. We yak about boot heels and lighters, what
the missus wont do in bed, the glass ceiling above St. John's,
about some fucker that needs a smack, about what the old
man said, that time. I say dont be a stranger. But because he
lives so handy, and lately paints, we never find the time to
live like that – tea and cigarettes and talk. (Are you living the
way you hoped you could be? Sometimes I feel easier, more
in control when I'm destroying myself and wearing down
the people around me.) For the hundredth time I want to
tell him to stop renting those cheapy fuckin Sci-Fi flicks,
to shove *House of Hate* down his throat, *The Devils, Dead
Souls.* Just please, for fuck sakes dont lose your footing, dont
let yourself sink in. But he could squat in Old Montreal,
inhaling cheap wine and spewing shite art, scale the predawn
steps of St. Joseph's every other day on bleeding knees and
we might know each other the same.

One Night in Scilly Cove

A fireman lets him sit up in the front,
flick some buttons and wear the hat.
I took a picture.

Down by the breakwater we watch two tomcats
scrap it out.
I'm rooting for the calico,
the boy just wants them to stop.

We mosey about the wharf
where the water is black tar
and grave and cruel.

I hook my finger through his little belt loop
while he drops rocks over the side.
If he were to fall in,
without hesitation, I'd follow.
I would not let him go off
to that other place
alone.

Ten minutes left before the shop closes,
he picks the biggest ice cream they've got.
The grey pony follows us
from her side of the fence.
The boy reaches out for my hand,
wants to know
where cold shivers come from.
It's what happens, I tell him,
when a goose walks over your grave.
He doesnt ask me to elaborate.

We stop and listen to a deep and distant trickle,
I tell the boy an old troll is having his one long annual pee.
He stares down through the grate for a time,
tells the troll he's not afraid,
then we run howling up the dirt road
in a fit of teary giggles.

The boy on the couch beneath the oil lamp,
fiddling with the transistor.
The constant static unsettling, somehow.

Kettle on the boil, my mind grinds
against the things I wish I could write
and the likelihood of some townie ponce
with clean clothes and careful fingernails
flirting with my girl this very moment.
Her loving it.

All the things I havent told her
come rising up to choke me
as I scorch my thumb on the handle
of a cast iron pan.
I burst out with an onslaught of filth
and the boy starts in sniffling,
familiar gloss in his eyes,
one fat tear streaking down his dusty cheek.

I'm sorry, I say,
I shouldnt have said those words.
It's not that, he says.
I was just thinking about stuff.
Like what sort of stuff?
I dont know, like what if
something was to happen to Mama

or what if St. John's disappeared?
What if a big wave came and we went back and it was all gone?
It's just that, you say, everybody
is supposed to get old and die.
And someday you'll be gone and Mom will be gone
and maybe I'll be out here on my own.

Sounds like someone
had too much ice cream.

Ill-Famed

Caught the stench of our old schemes on the lower road
last night. Like a thin flame dancing across my knuckles.
I was out wandering again, staring down strangers, jacket
fastened, belted, pockets zipped tight. I had a knife in my
jeans and I wanted to stick it somewhere. It's a hard-earned
talent, this skulking business. To do it convincingly you
have to be prepared for results that dont quite cast you in a
favourable light. From the top of some sultry stairway in a
town far off your chart, you should expect someday to be
referred to as a classist shit disturber. You should expect tight
circles of bloodthirsty city folk to have narrow discussions
about what you meant when you came in with that hard left.
About where you stand and therefore what you really stand
for. They'll probe your stats, scrutinize your photograph and
fret over the uselessness of damp facecloths while the blood
that dries onto your face blackens. By the time their fuckin
designated drivers arrive they'll have decided once more that
you simply missed your mark, that you hadnt the grit or the
gusto to push the task through to its end. And this will be as
close to the real truth as any of them will ever come.

You'll find yourself on some cool August night, crouched
over the fire pit, jabbing at the shadows, drenched with spite,
balls deep in a one-sided squabble about why that fist wasnt
raised fast enough, why that blade hadnt seen stone nor steel
at the start of the evening or why the phantom odour of a
long-abandoned pipe dream still lingers about the gutters of
your favourite stomping grounds, gloating, triumphant, chest
puffed out like an ill-famed prizefighter who has never had
the guts or the empathy to step inside the ring.

Old Skully

I spy one high on the wall
tucked between the schooners and pythons.
It's the price that catches my eye.

Scrutinize the rickety grin,
the dangling cigarette,
foggy black fedora shading the hollow
dead eye sockets
and that beautiful curl of blue-green smoke
bending across the brim.
One gold tooth.
That face was made for my arm.

I tell the fat shifty bastard
indeed I am sixteen,
and I have not been drinking.
He reaches for a blade, lecturing me
on the immorality
of blotting up young drunks.

The outline is the worst of it.
There's a lot of blood,
a pain so ridiculously fine
he might as well bang it in with a carpet knife.
He tells me to stop clenching like a girl.
I tell him, no, no,
I like it just well enough.

He smells like old spaghetti and stove ash.

Between the outline
and the colouring in

he looks around his cluttered place
for somewhere to lay his tissue,
then lifts his scruffy gut
and tucks the tissue there.
No one ever believes that part.

At my girlfriend's house,
playing cards and eating macaroni,
Old Skully is swollen on my throbbing forearm,
glistening with Vaseline.
Her father sees what I've done,
laughs in his lofty manner
in front of his weight-lifting pal,
says it's a fine tattoo, just fine,
that I'm gonna be so proud of it someday.
He shakes his head at his daughter
as if to say, as if to say…

When he finally fucks off downstairs
I light up a smoke at the table
and will not put it out when she asks.

Conflict of Interest

Those days my grandfather worked part-time as a night guard at the Ferryland lock-up. He was up past eighty then and had a reputation among the local drunks and hard tickets, who found themselves from time to time under his watch, for being fair and decent and discreet. It's been said he rarely confiscated a man's cigarettes and was likely to offer you a little nip if you weren't the rowdy type. He informed new faces that the only reason the cops gave him the job was not a man on the Shore could take him in a square go. Then he'd bore you off to sleep with long-winded war stories and rants about Joey Smallwood.

I always thought it'd be a good laugh if ever I were brought in while he was on duty. Not so. He went to the grave insisting that I still owed him a night's pay. No matter how often I helped mend the fences at the top of the meadow, or burnt myself to a blistered mess in the sun scraping and painting the clapboard on his house, he never let it go.

Now, I've been known to grumble that I was seized that night simply for standing and bleeding. But the truth, I suppose, is that I was full to the gills with Russian Prince and Valium and had descended upon the dance hall like a sudden southern squall of boot heels and dog chains and hee-haw warrior whoops.

Within minutes of my appearance outside the hall, the mad rumour spread that I'd head-butted a Trepassey girl and knocked her down on the ice and then tripped and fell on top of her and tried to kiss her.

I dont believe it myself, but I suppose you could say I'm slightly biased. I do remember slipping. I do recall a pretty face, and not having been kissed in a good way in a long time.

Next there's a scuffle, a nasal mainland twang, then the warm bath ambience of my forehead splitting open and cartoon stars and thin scarlet droplets sprinkled across the snow like the first thirty seconds of a fake Pollack piece. (Days later I found out the bastard was visiting from the Miramichi and wore a gold ring as big as my eyeball. But I was quick to forgive since I'd just finished reading *Lives of Short Duration*, and so counted myself lucky to be alive.)

When I come to again I'm propped against the side of the dance hall and my ex's little sister is messing with my buckle and licking the blood from the corner of my eye. Then it's the law dogs, right on cue. I'm standing there bleeding, nursing a crimson snowball to my face, my pants undone, the girl suddenly scarce as her big sister's affections. I'm too dazed to put up a fight.

In the back seat I get that patronizing third degree, the gloating tone. The cop leaves me to stew while he checks the dance hall for more unsavoury types. It takes me a full minute to realize that the little Plexiglas window, the one that separates the good guys from thc bad, the back seat from the front, has been left wide open. I can feel my legend swelling to rival my forehead as I slip my jacket off.

For a tight, cruel moment it seems that my shoulders wont fit, but I work out a method. The hips are tricky too, and I remember thinking how I wont have to worry about knocking up anyone's daughter anytime soon. Then it's the boots, one at a time. Bloody hand on the handle, the heavy Crown Vic door tumbling open and I'm off like a jackrabbit across the icy parking lot, a blundering feral scramble into the surrounding woods, my good old jacket still in the back seat.

They picked me up thumbing about an hour later, halfway between Renews and civilization. The cop stood outside the car with my jacket slung over his shoulder and asked me if I was cold enough yet. The blast of heat coming from the dash. I got in. What odds.

Long dawdling ride to the station and the cop saying how he heard I was good at literature and that I read books. He asked me if I've ever read Salinger. I asked him if he knew that Salinger drank his own piss and whipped his dogs. He said he heard I was into artists and paintings, so why was I going around smashing things? He wanted to know where all the hash was coming from lately, said maybe if I knew a thing or two about a thing or two he could just drop me home instead of locking me up. I told him what to lick, and how to go about it. He got a kick out of that, then radioed in my name and the situation I was in. After a time the pencil pusher on the other end squelched back to say that my grandfather was on duty and wasnt that a conflict of interest? The cop in the front seat looked back at me and grinned, then replied that my grandfather would have to be dismissed for the night.

I got the lowdown on *The Hitchhiker's Guide to the Galaxy* the rest of the way to the station. I just sat there smearing blood into the seat cushions.

My old grandfather was on his way down the steps while the cop was leading me through the station doors. I was having trouble walking, Valium sloshing around in my knees. My shirt was black with blood. It was flaking from my face and head, crisped into my hair. Grandfather didnt look too pleased. He was hunched under the weight of his old 50s biker jacket. He had his lunch tin, a dog-eared Louie L'Amour tucked under his arm and his boots were untied, like he'd slipped them on in a hurry.

He buckled the belt on his jacket, looked me up and down, tossed me the battered western and told me in his low gravelly way that I owed him a night's pay. I told him goodnight, but my grandfather never answered.

As the cop was leading me to my cell I tossed the book in the garbage can near his desk. I dug around for it the next morning, but it was gone.

Better Served

Dirty, slippery, underhanded, late night bastard impulse. The urge bubbles up after months of slumber, and in the fever to scratch it down (when he might be better served mending a fence, raising a scaffold, or levelling off a foundation plot) he's only half ashamed of how much it means to him.

Structuring the goddamn thing: which word goes where and which phrase deserves a line unto itself. All building toward that surplus insight, dead weight of wordy drivel that ties up all the loose ends of his compulsion. Self-serving itch to put pen to paper. But there's no amount of scratching, no. This compulsion is nothing more than mockery, taunting him with the fact that he might be driven to do this for the rest of his breathing days. And that his life can be too easily whittled down to a shadowy collection of impractical, harebrained, idealistic flashes that take him nowhere except into the tired arms of yet another hopeful *story* that will likely never see the true light of day.

He will always pine for workers hands. Because what boils up in the blood sometimes can spook him into wanting something solid. Wanting something measurable, something that comes with a manual. Wanting.

Because he knows in his heart of hearts that what's transferred from pencil to page is oftentimes a shame against the calluses his hands cannot lay claim to.

Book
Burnings

The Hammer

This was the dry bitter middle of February down at the smoke shack
outside that *place* in Scarborough
and I was trying to keep myself to myself, to let the thick sweet tea
work its way to my bloodstream,
but this arsehole with a gooey pink scar across the back of his hand
put there by his drunken father's razor,
this *dude* who wanted everyone to call him the Hammer
and laugh at his titty jokes,
who had an aura of oozing black rotting meat, something you'd uncover beneath
the floorboards of a burned out warehouse
or stuffed in the closet in an abandoned motel,
he kept staring at me with that dark starving dullness
and asking me how I slept
and how I was coming along
and how much longer I had
and how bad I'd bottomed out
before jumping on the abstinence train. And there I was,
stalling for words, fighting back the bully in me,
my brain numb with recovery jargon,
sipping my tea and sucking on a cigarette that kept going out.

He leaned in with his lighter and told me how one of his many ex-girlfriends
– because she got so pissed off
with her smokes burning away to nothing in the ashtray –
came up with a sort of idea that had to do with how the tobacco was packed
and how *she's* the reason behind my cigarette going out
because she put a call in to Imperial Tobacco and they got right on it.

But they never paid her a cent
or mentioned her name, the fuckers.
So he says, Next time your cigarette goes out you can think on her.

She had amazing tits, he said.

It was his third time in that same *place*
in under three years.
Cocaine, tequila, party pills, strippers,
all the bullshit that comes along with it.

Nowadays, many hours and days and months from there,
I think on the Hammer when my cigarette goes out
and I touch the tight scar on my forehead
and I daydream about whipping my old man
and I think on this kid I used to *crucify* back home,
years ago, for no good reason,
and I wonder where he is
and I wonder where the Hammer is
and who he's tormenting
and whether or not
we can smell people's souls
when they're at their lowest,
their most desperate end.

I Wont Go Into Detail

My little sister's brought the police to my house.
Nothing new for this part of town,
but there are two policemen out there now
standing like humans in my living room.

They, the police,
have just come from the apartment my folks rent in town
(to be close to the situation with my sister)
where they forced the door in
because they were led to believe she might be in there
on the floor
bleeding to death
on account of the so-called boyfriend.

(I wont go into detail.
It's a messy affair of
hidden cameras
psychic hysteria
sleep deprivation
sawn-off crack-barrels
bugged telephones
and bogus birth dates.)

My folks are away down South
(reprieve from the situation with my sister)
and now, to maybe spare my father
another premature grey
and because I am the black sheep with a youth record
stretching from here to Gormon's Hill,
I might go and fix their door
before they get back to the Island.

Maybe I should go over and clean the place out,
right down to the toilet paper on the roll,
spray-paint something lewd and cryptic
on their walls
and take a dirty big steaming shit
in the middle of their living room floor.

I have my excuses, I suppose;
my youth jammed into garbage bags
and slung out over the doorstep,
told to go rob gas stations,
to sell dope,
to suck old men's cocks,
all because
I brought the law dogs to the door…again.

Still, I cant recall them ever swinging round
with their battering ram on my account.

The boys in bl(ack)
out there right now
in my living room.
I slink my way close
to the warm little bag of T-3s
on the kitchen counter.
The old timer of the two
hasnt yet taken his hand from the butt of his gun
and the younger pup picks a piece of lint
from his body armour
while my sister cries wretched madhouse tears.

I *Wont* Go Into Detail

By the way, he's from away. Not from around here. Death-
black eyes, a foreign straight-razor maze of far-flung streets,
outlandish foods and fanciful textures. He's known so many,
bored stiff with the Promised Land.

She's from right here, born and reared right here. Never
been anywhere. Came down with the measles that time and
missed her flight and her cheeks still burn whenever anyone
mentions Alberta.

He's not from around here, faintly tinted accent, solid
gold bouncer's ring as shifty as the next four months' rent,
cologne thick as a cloud of locusts, first name blazoned
across his buckle, flashing in the strobes like some confused
distress signal from a vessel whose crew has no clue how
close to the rocks they already are.

And so happens, tonight, she's taking all comers, her purse
gone astray in a bathroom stall, girlfriend fucked off with
that oilrig fella and the Southern Comfort seething in her
blood like the sum of too many near misses all raged up into
this glorious horrible night on the town.

And everything shimmers from the ankles to the crown.

I Never Dream of My Father
(for Leo's boys)

Byron dreams of his father
since he's passed.

In Byron's dream his father is mending
the eave of a ramshackle house no one lives in.
His father leans out
gravely, beyond his equilibrium,
pounding felt nails in place with his bare fist.
Byron holds against the crumbling chimney
an eight ounce hammer made for a child.
His coveralls are too big.
He waits to hand his father another board.
When he tries to lift the cordless Skilsaw
he finds it's too heavy, the handle greasy.
His hands are cold,
his fingers not quite filling out
the heavy canvas work gloves he wears.
He fumbles the saw,
as it tumbles over the edge of the roof
he watches in petrified disgrace.
As an afterthought,
long since the saw has fallen,
his father reaches out for it, lunging,
braced against nothing but air.
He disappears beyond the edge of the eave,
making no sound.

That's all, Byron says, that's the dream.
Not much to it, really.

Birthday Greetings

Seventeen kilometres in
and I'm still juggling the fire.
Cant say if that's a good sign
or a bad.
Blood soaking through my socks.
I pluck one thought
from the thunder in my head:
burn the little house to the ground,
scorch it flat and wait for him
to come hulking across the meadow
with his feeble bucket,
from there, take him by the shoulders,
force his eye,
offer the nod
and if he cant account for the absence of warmth,
if he still insists that it was not cold,
then I will mash his teeth down his fuckin throat.

Another voice contends
that I'm needed elsewhere,
but I drown it out with another shot,
lean into the horseshit wind while the coppers cruise
slowly past, eyeing my drunken hooded swagger
that's slowly giving over to a limp.

There is, thankfully,
no law that sees inside the heart.

They double back, they always do,
and I sling the flask into the gutter
as they approach.
Slender young lady cop in the driver's seat,

grizzled old dinosaur oblivious in the passenger seat.
Everything okay, she asks. Have you been drinking?
I say yes, I've been drinking
since I was a child.
She wants some identification. I ask her what for,
but she just stares grimly
and I dont want her kind of trouble today.

She inspects my card.
Happy birthday, she says, you're Christ's age today.
I say yes, and we all know what they done to him.
She hands me back my card.
Are you an actor or a writer
or something?
I say no, no, not today.
Where are you headed?
To visit my father.
How did you cut your hand?
I glance down at the thick black ooze
crusting between my knuckles.
I want to tell her
I gnawed myself.
I was defending someone's right to expire.
I want to tell her of the child I freed
from the jaws of a beast.
I cut myself on the back bumper of an old mustang
I helped a couple of hooligans jumpstart
about a half hour behind me.

It sounds like a decent story, once it's out,
but she doesnt buy it.
She eyeballs me some more
and I try not to stagger back
under the heft of her reservations.

When they've rounded the far turn
I scoop the flask up out of the gutter
and drain the final quarter. My guts burn.

I'm getting old and that voice again,
scrawny and fragile and *not here*,
pleading with me to turn back and get on with it,
get on with it.

But I carry on southeast, like the fool I am,
only forty-five kilometres to go,
blood and sweat and blister juice
sloshing,
already fancying the heat
from the inferno I will make
of that shack of that long ago time.

Frank's Old Bedroom

I call out to the boy.
It takes a minute to remember
I'm alone in the house,
alone with someone else's years.
I snarl at the darkness –
Well, come slit my throat.
Flip the feather pillow
for the cool, fictitious comfort,
appraise each breath, give a nod
to the Big Guy, up there,
but cant find my way back down.

It's that nakedness
for the weak
for the outcast
for the old.
Like dropping the boy at school:
the breakfast rush, the uniform battle
brush hair teeth face and hands
the boots the coat the mitts the hat –
Come on come on, you can play later.
Play later.
Did you take your lunch?
Where's the blue folder?

Onward to the cluster of more industrious parents,
the scarred frames of lockers, the indoor shoes,
squawks and flaps of little people, free as gulls.

He races up the stairs
to meet the morning prayers –
the anthem and the Ode –

and I suddenly miss him fiercely
because he's driven my every waking thought so far this day.

Now I gotta think for myself.

Raw slippery day ahead.
Like waking to a bump
in the black of night,
and not fearing for your own self
because the noise has likely come
from the house across the meadow,
from further down the road,
across the harbour,
lands away,
ricocheted from another time.

But still the lurking tension
that someone out there doesnt even know they need your help.

More Scar than Spider

Two weeks, two hundred miles offshore, I'm fourteen
pounds lighter by the time we land in Cape Broyle. Spew up
rancid bacon grease the moment I hit the safety of the wharf.
The sky wont stop tumbling, rolling, sinking. Cook tells me
to focus on the harbour, the swell out there, to avoid looking
at dry land until it passes. Land sick! he shouts to the crew.
I'm mocked and jeered. I want to smack that dirty old cunt
so bad.

Collect half my pay and hightail it to my new girlfriend's
place. I'm already waiting in her room with a bottle of lotion
when she gets home from school and within minutes her
mother catches her straddling me, my hand tucked down
the back of her jeans. But I've got more money than I've
ever had in my life, and we both laugh at her mother. We
hit the road for St. John's. Friday evening and there's a motel
out there somewhere and a friend's spare room and Ches's
French fries and dirty bars where no one knows anything
about anything at all.

And the Black Rose Tattoo Shop.

My mind is bent on a baby scallop shell with the words *never
again* wrapped around it in old school scroll. The fat man has
nothing of the sort in his folders or on his walls. He's never
seen a scallop. I tell him they're best raw, fresh from the shell
while the muscle still has a twitch left in it. He draws up a
foolish, crude mockery of my last two weeks of misery and
torture. It's cartoonish and hard to trust so I decide on a
nickel-sized black widow spider. I want to bang it in the soft
spot between my thumb and index finger, but the moment

he is to lay the stencil down my girlfriend shakes her head ever so faintly and I know it's a shitty idea so I flip my hand and let him stamp it on the underside of my wrist.

This one takes only twenty minutes, but I cannot understand the pain: like someone clamping down your hand while a cat rakes its claws across the part of the wrist stupid people try to slit. After the first few minutes my girl splits for the bar upstairs to wait it out. She doesnt need to see how tough I'm not.

Off to the Captain's Quarters then, for a room and a decent feed and all the other fine things you miss at sea.

A good six months to heal, and turns out to be more scar than spider, but it's forgivable, since he shined up Old Skully's gold tooth for free.

Letting it Pass

I cant let it pass, find myself asking the old bastard what
he's looking at me like that for. Like what? he says. Like
that, says me. I wasnt looking any which way, says he. Well,
alls I'm saying, and I'm trying to be as civil as possible,
I'm not trying to be disrespectful or anything, but alls
I'm saying is that you gave me a look, and, maybe since
you gave it then you never saw it, but, since I was on the
receiving end, I'm saying I saw it. That's all. Maybe I'm a
bit ragtag today, but I dont like to be looked at like I was
some kind of scum. Now I'm trying to be civil, you have
to understand. That's what's wrong with all this, says the
old timer, as he flicks his butt end at a flock of pigeons,
that's why the parish is gone to hell – common civility.
So fuck off, he says I'll look at you and anyone that looks
like you any which way I wants to.

Bottom Drawer

It's the bedroom drawer again,
the bottom one,
cesspit of dirty yearnings,
scandalous stains of stolen foods –
apple cores, prune pits,
skins of a garlic clove,
morsel of baker's chocolate –
sinister remnants
of my insatiably evil appetite.

He's pointing
at something in the drawer.
I press my memory for it now,
this fresh atrocity.
I want it to be something worthy:
spent box of Seadog matches,
a cousin's severed finger,
neighbour girl's bloody underwear.
But it wont materialize,
this wrong he's motioning at,
just the heft of his meaty hand
gripped tight to the back of my neck,
forcing me to look
at what new horror
I've tried to hide.

He wants to know
when is all this gonna stop?
He cant comprehend
why I would do such a thing.
And when, he roars,

when are things gonna change
around here?

I dont know, I dont know.
My left shoulder is numbing out.
I can hear the gang up in the meadow.

There are no more specifics.
Unclean, unnatural, deviant,
that's all I'm left with.

Apparently

He's a drunk, into the downers.
He "struggles" with it though.
Oh yeah, he works on it.
He's never been ejected by force, no,
but warned, second-hand,
not to come back.
Best kind, when he's sober.
But you cant even catch his eye some days.
He's well read,
if you're into that sort of thing.
I think he's half queer. Didnt you hear about him
and what's-his-face
outside that pub that night, and buddy was crying?
Oh yeah, they says he had a hard old go,
but that dont excuse him from kicking parking meters
and smashing bottles and going around
punching brick walls. Hit me, I told him, hit me.
Or that's what I felt like saying.

Someone said something to him one time,
about how much they liked what he does,
and he told buddy right where to go.
How's that for a man of letters?
Sure, he's got a little fella too.
Something now, a grown man going around
badmouthing his own bloodline,
and he with that little fella who thinks his dad can do no wrong.
Anyhow, they're all fucked up, that crowd,
from up that way.

To the Punk Who Robbed My Girlfriend's Purse

Suffering fuck, next thing you know I'll be chalking it
up to *karma*, and can only assume you'll be back some
night to bash my living room window out. I was that
kind of punk: big black boots, too cool to wear a warm
hat, skulking anger stalking only forward.

Ah Christ, you got me all sentimental now, thinking
about the time I hacked down old Jack R's crabapple
tree with his own hatchet. That tree bore the finest
apples on the Shore. He guarded it with his life, not to
mention that prehistoric double-barrel salt gun. But
I chopped it down in early May while he was in St.
Clare's for open-heart surgery. I was that kind of punk.
Not creepy-crawly slithering city boy. I drank like a
tornado and I still have all my teeth.

Listen here, arsehole, it's hardly the $230.00, that's fuck
all, that's just groceries and lights and phone. It's hardly
the extremely rare, fuckin irreplaceable vintage leather
purse from Colorado. It aint the old black and white of
her and Koko. And it aint the keys to the front door that
had her in panic mode for a week, me tearing my Jesus
hair out, her mother forking over to the locksmith. It's
more or less the fact that you are out there somewhere
counting yourself lucky. You goddamn punk.

Now you got me all sappy, thinkin about the time
I led a pack of dogs onto a campsite in some fuzzy
provincial park and stole everything that wouldnt burn.
Rummaging through the contents of a red cooler,
I found eggs, bread, white rum, steaks, syringes and a

little Zip-lock bag labelled *Jimmy's Insulin*. I pocketed the booze and the steaks and tossed the rest into the bushes. We ate the steaks raw. A month later I drank Pine-Sol to kill my tapeworm. I was that kind of punk.

The Writer at the Bar

He was flipping through that book, one of the ones the Russians banned, where the poet (disgraced) plummets from the pedestal and realizes in one vivid, liberating instant that nothing he's ever written is worth reading or repeating, that it's all been bullshit. All of it. Bull*shit*. After all the handshakes, plagiarized dedications and applause, after all the drawn-out, soggy codeine nights of getting it down, getting it out, getting it said – well, there is nothing that he could have said that's not already been snatched up and far more elegantly set down by superior thinkers, greater minds from more pliable times. And worse, that even had he gotten there first, had he been born into one of the decades he's longed for, he would still be this, he would still be this, and this and this. This.

Still, rumour has it he's behaved in a ghastly manner before the cultured ones. That has to count for something? They say he's repented, refashioned his ways to help the pretense along. He's fallen back, done commendable things for those who take and take and take. He's dismissed the ones he does not understand, and glorified the ones who could have done better with a kick in the goddamn mouth. Squandered the talent, of course. That's gotta count for something?

Divvied out slices of his self, the past, heart, balls, to this town, the old town and the new town. Niggardly, acidic, half-rotted slices peddled in a different time, through a different hunger. Morsels that are now being spat back in his face as he flips through the passages of another chapter he cant remember writing.

Then the ones who despise the way he's overcome, and the eager gin-soaked palms swish swish swishing together, the breathless gossip yearning for his ultimate fall. All a matter of course, so he's told. But Christ, how he caters to them all, how he still carves off the best of him yet to satiate the bland palates of the castaway users and takers and bitchers and castrated would-be Don Quixotes. How he keeps going back to scream: Look at me! *Look* at me! I'm still here, I'm still this... This. This. This.

Hey, come on, come on, he says, remember that bloke in that book by that English fella, how he bottomed out because he didnt have the right kind of money smell? You dont remember? No bother. Just dont get so up in arms. Here is no great *matter*. Come on, come on, he says, buy me another. Put it on your tab and I'll scratch you into my next one. How's that sound?

Smoking in Bed

There's a cross, brushed metal cross
in a church in Winnipeg
lately weeping a sort of oily residue.
Hundreds have been making pilgrimage
every day for a month
to witness with their own eyes,
but no one can say just yet
if it constitutes a miracle or not.

A lady, last week, was distressed
to have found a human bone
on a beach on Fogo Island.
It's since been determined
the bone is from an animal,
although what type of animal
no one seems to know.

I'm smoking in bed again tonight,
cajoling a stubby pencil across
another drooping page.
Even though I know
they're eventually coming for me,
I'm hell-bent on the softest path
to the end of this line,

and not an ash, not an ash
has yet to hit the sheets.

Make Your Peace

My sister calls to say I'd better get in to the hospital and make my peace. Grandfather's on his way out. Havent seen him for eighteen months. Stopped visiting. I couldnt abide having to pretend I was my father just so he could, in good conscience, gobble up the apple flip I brought him. Our last conversation was set in the thirties or forties, something to do with the only man left who could properly shoe a horse, and how long it took to walk from Ferryland to St. John's and back again. He recommended a good barber on Duckworth Street who offers a decent trim and shave, hot towel treatment, the works, for a dollar ten. I laughed and told him the days of the straight razor were long come and gone, especially at that price. He looked at me for a long time, then pointed at the scuffed toes of my boots and shook his head. An orderly spoke to him like the way the workers speak to toddlers in a daycare centre. My grandfather rolled his eyes and called me Gary and I left.

My tough old grandfather there in a hospital bed with the flesh drum tight about his skull. His eyes are open, full of the same blue sky, but not obliged to this world. And here's my father sitting at the bedside with the back of his hand on my grandfather's cheek. I havent seen him in maybe eighteen months either. He tells me how Grandfather slipped and broke his hip. *He's not strong enough for surgery… Hasnt been sensible in a while… Morphine, ya know… He would have liked to know you were here…*

Grandfather stirs discreetly when the priest comes in. Last rites, a few kind words from the good Father, and before the door swings shut behind him my grandfather breathes his last. And there it is, that moment when the light leaves the eyes. It's true. It's a truth. I look to the wretched ceiling tiles, around the stagnant room, cross over to the window and scour the distant tree line. My grandfather is not anywhere.

It's the first I've seen my father cry. I press the back of my hand against his cheek and tousle his hair a little and try to think of something lasting and wise to say. Glance down to my feet and note the boots could do with a good polish.

Apparently

For now you get to be nothing but warmth, a
kindly, kindred recess to fold into. You get to be a
scent, an idea of shelter, neutral god with no track
record and no master plan. For now you do not
come up short. But this ten-pound bundle cradled
in your nervous arms, as though there were a
thousand-foot drop beneath you, will one day turn
to you and tell you to go fuck yourself. And you
will have earned that.

Old School (Dublin, March 1999)

I hear the man with the needle say
that if he did *that* every time
he'd be out of business in a month.
Then something erupts,
something about wanting to see
the tip fresh out of the bag.

   – But they've been scrubbed down
with this special brush, see?
Soaked in the best solution,
bagged and autoclaved,
tubes, barrels, tips, inside and out.
Look, all the excess ink is gone.
That's where the poison is, not the needle.
The bad stuff lingers in the ink,
and I dump any unused portion
in between jobs, always.
But needles, new needles every time?
I'd be done for in a month.
Now, if you dont like the way we roll
you can find some place else.

There is a tense quiet for a time, then laughter.
One or the other done time with the other's cousin.
There comes talk about old school outlines.
The man with the needle wants to try his hand
at some New Age shadow effect,
offers a discount if he arses it up.
Then that urgent, deranged, twanging fly buzz of the gun.

Lucy's Apron

I'd spent my day chopping the heads off live ones, slurping cold spawn from my wrists and forearms, slinging dead lances at the rival pickers and aiming slimy by-catch (sea rats mostly) down the front of Lucy's apron. I doubt I even made two pans all day and it's a safe bet that more than one skipper was wishing for days bygone when they could've tossed me into the sludge barge or winched me out over that sneering school of dogfish Dinny'd allegedly spotted circling the wharf at daybreak.

Lucy had seven pans in by ten oclock. She hadnt taken her eyes from the table or spoken a harsh word except to tell Martin J. to go home to his mother's tit. We'd all heard the story of Thursday's sticky three oclock fumbling behind the smoke shack, how Lucy'd come bumming for a cigarette and readily agreed to some gummy tradeoff. We all knew Martin J. was near-on bad as Dinny when it came to the bullshit. And we all knew Lucy, with her allergies and asthma, but it was too good a tall one not to let it have its way; Lucy's lusty abandon blazing in our heads like chicken pox fever. And besides, didnt it fit right in with the time Rodney's wife got caught with her head in the priest's lap?

Come on Lu-lu, me and you, break time in the twine shed. Hey Lucy, you got something on your cheek there, cream or something, I dont know... Lucy! Dont be so stingy with it, come on, round for the b'ys...

Once, during the ambush, she dared, with a sort of shrouded, half-expectant plea creased in her brow, to glance my way. She stayed with her cousins at the end of my road and had lent me the gloves I was wearing.

The Very Back Room

Surprise Visit

Daybreak by the time I slunk back to the house to find my black truck gone, front door unlocked, dishes washed and a half flask of vodka front and centre in the fridge.

My first move was to barricade the front door with the big leather chair, some boards from out back, the coffee table and the fifty-seven pound suitcase I'd yet to unzip.

Having my truck gone wasnt much fun, mostly because I didnt know if some skeet from the street had been scoping me while I was off on a jag and decided to jack it, or if someone who loved me, wanting to make a statement about the condition I was in, had made off with it to see if I'd resurface. Maybe the boy's mother, maybe my buddy from the newsroom.

But I figured it wasnt likely that some arsehole had busted in and done my dishes, left my vodka behind, *then* fucked off with my truck.

I made some phone calls, reinforced the front door. Took my vodka out to the back shack, dug out a half bottle of white rum from the ceiling boards, poured the vodka into the rum, got the guitar on the go, plucked out Springsteen's *Nebraska* and waited for the shit storm.

I stank like something I shouldnt have. Knuckles a swollen mangle of crusty scabs, and I was throwing up bloody bile in an empty paint can when I heard my truck rumbling up the road.

These Rooms

These days there are these rooms
I find myself wincing
in the corners of,
scrutinizing my cobbler's handiwork,
scraping motorcycle grease
from beneath my nails
with a blade as dull as my new-found
Saturday nights.

Once in a while I huff,
nod, cock my head, snort,
slap my breast pocket,
tug my collar, pick at a button,
glance at the faces
as they talk and talk and talk.

It's all about the message,
the warning,
the cautionary tale.
Take heed young man. This one
lost the job, the woman,
the two boys, the dog
and every friend in the world.

This man's been *out* for three years
but now he's been back for three days
and it's still the same out there,
only colder somehow.
Suicide, he says, feels more reasonable
the older I get.
When he finishes
a lackluster quiet takes over.

How to talk about waking at 3am to the dog's low growl,
her forepaws planted on the windowsill,
eyes fixed on something flitting through the meadow
at the edge of my land?
How to talk about the back of my neck
as I fumble through the terror
to light a lamp,
to let whatever is out there know
that the house is conscious at present
and not accepting visitors.

How to talk about trying to find the words
to negotiate
with whatever is not at rest here on my land,
stuttering through the declarations,
the mantras, the affirmation
that I come not only in peace
but in search of peace as well,
that though I might be loud
and naked at times
and do mad things with fire,
I'm one of the good guys,
nonetheless.

Next, old Paddy tells how
he was driving too slow down
Merry Meeting Road
last Wednesday night
and some meathead in a meat-eating Ford
was in such a hurry to get somewhere special
that he followed Paddy into the Sobey's parking lot
to let Paddy know
what a slow cunt he is.
Anyways, Paddy says,

there but for the grace of God
go I.

I used to hang a towel
over the bathroom mirror, someone says,
so I wouldnt have to look at myself.
Remember when, someone says.
Easy does it, says another.
We're only as sick as our secrets…
First thing's first…
Keep the plug in the jug…
Wherever you go, there you are…

I sit here, these days, in these rooms,
because they say it is the easier, softer way.
If I'm asked to speak
I mention how grateful I am to be where I am
and to have what I have.
And I'm careful not to address
my own reasons for shunning the mirror
past a certain hour,
how it's shag-all to do with any distress
with myself or where I've come from,
but more to do with what the dog is tapped into.
More to do with
who or what might be there,
loitering in the candlelight,
smug doppelgänger
over my shoulder in the mirror –
sinful scene from my elementary days,
gauzy face pressed against the windowpane,
old Frank with his bottle of Young's,
tracing a shrewd finger
round the rim
of his favourite glass.

Duluoz

All right, cut the shit, old codger, this is dried out, twice strained roach butt tobacco, bomber weed stashed in the hollowed out bedpost of the best fuck in town. It's a beat up, jerk stained, rusted getaway car with no brakes. Antique armchair idling in the attic heckling the cobwebs, the mildew and the mould.

Settle down, Skipper, this is baked beans, black coffee and burnt toast for a slothful, over-talkative midnight breakfast. It's a pocketful of apples slipping out the back door.

Lookit here, gaffer, this is a real lead pencil, a feather pen. It's a typewritten mutiny dying to slam that pedal down. Cluttered up, withdrawn and explosive, it's a battered first edition of *Tortilla Flat* buckled sideways in some arsehole's back pocket. It's the great French Canadian bank robbery.

Keep your gloves on, Methuselah, this is strong thick cheap red wine. It's the hair on the back of your neck. Hot bead of vagrant's blood trickling down the blade of the last decent straight razor in town. This is rough, natural grain we're talking about; no finish.

Listen up, old-timer, there's a trip across the goddamn country at the drop of a hat, at the turn of a page.

Buckle up, big fella, there's a madman at the wheel, watching your every move.

Believer

He puts me in mind of my old grandfather when
I spot him hobbling in the fog past Exit 31, spritely, in red
lumberjack plaid, buckled under the burden of his seventy
odd years.

He calls himself Zeke. His forearm is as thick as my neck
and when I accept his gargantuan hand in mine I realize,
obediently, that he could easily rip my whole arm off if
things were to go amiss.

We spark up some smokes. A story comes on the radio
about a fresh scandal at the Vatican. It seems now that
even the pope knew a thing or two about who was
doing what to who, back in the day. I switch it off when
old Zeke bats at the rosary dangling from my rear-view
mirror. He asks if I believes in God. I tell him yes, I've
been known to utter a scatter prayer.

Listen here, he says, if you wants to know about prayer,
sure my own wife lost her left tit to the old breast
cancer, yes sir she did, and didnt I and me daughter just
get right down and pray for near on two years. And not
them novena type ones neither, no no, this here I'm
talking about is *praying*, young feller, praying. And do you
know what? Well I wasnt much of a believer back then,
I just went along with things for the women's sake, you
know, but you know what? Well the wife's tit came back,
anyhow. That's all I'll say about it. Nipple and all, yes, the
nipple came back too.

Is that right? Approaching Harbour Grace now, and I'm thinking he's more like my old grandfather than I first suspected.

Yes, he says, that's right. I knows it sounds like a crock, and like I said I wasnt much of a believer back then, but now I am. Now I prays every day whether things is good or bad or nothing at all. I prays all the time. And one thing I knows about Jesus, he says, Jesus is, he says… ahhh there's Pussy Rock, he says, pointing up to the cliffside across the bay.

Sure enough, midway up the side of the far cliff, there's a glossy, swollen mound of gulch rock, complete with slit and a tuft of damp bushes at the summit, and dont it bear a striking resemblance. Well. Christ.

Many a night, Zeke says, many a night I felt like crawling up the side of that mountain and tucking meself inside Pussy Rock, yes. Anyhow, what was I saying? Oh yes, prayer, that's right. Well the daughter too, see, her husband was a mean bastard with his fists you know, knocked her teeth out and whatnot, but sure she prayed and she prayed and she prayed every day for eighteen months, that there'd be an end put to it, and sure enough wasnt he crushed under some hydraulic thing up in Fort Mac? Squashed him flat it did. Closed casket, the works. And she down on her knees every day for eighteen months, like I said.

Now you tell me, he says, you tell me.

Mousey

It's Friday night, late,
I'm present and accounted for,
painting stripes on the cupboards in the porch.
The boy is sound asleep and Lime Street
is roaring, threatening something old in me.

There's a woman on my step,
late thirties, drugstore perfume and the clinging cigarette.
Are you Mousey? she goes.
I dont quite know how to respond to that,
glance down between my legs where my tail
might be curled.
She rolls onto her tiptoes
to scope out my porch.
I was told a little bluish house,
down from the shop, she goes.
I shake my head.
I was told there was a Mousey here?
He's… ahh… twenty-one.

She takes a step back and I see her
suddenly seeing me.
She crushes her cigarette
and the sparks blow beneath my truck,
winking out in a pool of mystery fluid
that's been leaking for weeks.
She lights another cigarette.

My daughter, she goes, my daughter is only fourteen.
She's fourteen, we were doing so good…
I cant help you, I say, but I hope she turns up.
Well, she mumbles, sorry.

Dont be, I say, dont be. That's your child.
I'd pound on every door
from here to Port Aux Basque
and I wouldnt apologize to a fuckin soul.
That's your child.

She smiles at that and squares her shoulders,
squints down Lime Street at the gaggle
of housing units below.
She pulls a black elastic from her wrist
and twists her hair into a bun.
Thanks, she goes, thanks for that.
She flings her half-smoked cigarette,
then stomps down the hill
thumping her fists off her thighs –
the shabby bedtime slippers
slapping a manic beat,
shattering car windows, headlights,
short-circuiting the streetlamps.
A shower of sparks rains down.
A screen door fails its hinges,
a tomcat howls.

Steal my way upstairs in the sudden dark,
peek in at the boy,
blankets tousled about his feet,
pillow slumped to the floor
beside his nightstand
and the brown fleece monkey
holding vigil at the edge of his mattress.

Counting the Blessings

Some nights when I'm lying there
counting the blessings
they tell us to count,
my head goes off to places
that make me feel both miniature
and quite considerable
in the imagining.

The old house is scorched flat,
all the vital papers inside,
in the drawer
in the very back room,
the leaden knick-knacks, surplus mementos
of bygone friendships –
all blistered to a crisp.

The old truck meets with a screeching
concrete end.
The boy in the full custody of his mama
living fully in Little Italy,
the books remaindered,
gathered into a dusty bin, en route
to the mulching plant.
The dog roaming the barrens
with a pack of coyotes, grizzled
and full of feral glory.
The woman snuggled in
with a bright-eyed farm boy out west,
tending the coop, her belly
swelling with number three.

And me on the GS750, sliding

beneath the wheels of a Midland semi,
coming to months later
in a sparkling sterile cot in some bordertown,
my face restructured, my memory
a dim fog of scribbles
and blunt cravings,
nothing in my pockets but a wad
of insurance cash
and a crisp, blank notebook
with not one wrinkle in the spine.

One Conscious Child

Gary, I say, that's my father's name. I dont know about you.
He laughs at this, squeezes the back of my neck so earnestly
I know I'm gonna feel it for a week. It's near on closing
and he's having a squabble with himself because all the old
ghosts have long since slithered off the edge.

He asks after my little fella, tells me I seem lighter and
heavier all the one time, then wanders back into his head for
a spell. Because all that matters now, he says, is who you'll
be when the nights fold in, when the rules no longer apply.

The barmaid pleads for last call and Gary roars so hard he
slips from his stool and taps his lip on the jagged corner of a
lotto machine. Thin, bloody spittle slides down his chin. He
tips his beer again, nails it, turns to me.

Looka here, Hynes, the only thing you can offer the world
is one conscious child. There's nothing else worth leaving
behind.

Gary says none of it matters, none of *this* matters unless that
little girl in Three Sands, Oklahoma is here at his deathbed
to hold his hand, tuck the stray hair back behind his ear,
place a cold cloth on his forehead, whisper something kind,
say something lasting and wise like – I think I'll hold off on
that thing I was telling you about. It just doesnt feel like the
right time.

Gary pounds his meaty fist, grandly raises his empty glass to
the man upstairs.

Lookit here, Hynes, I've conspired with ten thousand men but've only given two of em my phone number.
I drew a line and let it be known that whosoever crossed it would be fighting to the death. Aint these the walls we sometimes gotta raise? Anyways, fuck it. What does any of it matter? After seventeen years of scrapping it out, trying so Christly hard not to fall back, denying I ever was that kind of creature... ah fuck... go ask the girl with the southern drawl. Her heart dont even know it's pumping Newfoundland blood. Little soul in Three Sands who dont even know she's never been home...

I offer Gary a match but he declines.

Three weeks later I'm stopped at that bastard red light at the top of Long's Hill. The gage is on empty, the battery light keeps flashing, and be fucked if I ever wanna see or hear from any of those fuckers ever again.

From the backseat my little guy pipes up – Watch is asshole... asshole.

A whole minute passes.

That's not a very nice word. Who are you talking to?

The cars, he says, the cars.

Very well, I say, then slam that pedal when the light goes green.

Safe Place

Full dark and raining hard
by the time we pulled onto the upper road.
I'd been thinking I might burst into tears
at the sight of the house,
but I did not.
I sensed the looming presence
of something that did not want me here,
in my own home.

The key wouldnt take
and it pissed down the back of my neck
for ten minutes before
I worked the storm door open.
The inside knob was tied good.
I smashed a mineral water bottle
and slashed at the twine with the jagged neck
until it gave way.

If she'd seen what I'd seen
while crossing the barrens –
the galloping hoofed white creature
in the fog ahead of the truck,
faces of men long passed, wandering the roadside,
led astray by years,
the dead crow with the smashed beak
and grey scorched eyes perched on the bonnet,
its gaze never meeting mine –
well, I guess she'd be a little hesitant
to step inside the old house.

I played with a damp match for an unsuccessful minute,
checked the rooms in the dark.

In Frank's old bedroom I was greeted
by the comatose face of an age-shattered man
in the bed my boy sleeps in.
His eyes blind beyond the place
where the grief of seclusion
takes a human being.
His grey-green head seemed to roll
toward me as I entered.
He looked about to speak
so I bawled out like a youngster
and clapped my hands and pissed myself a little
running from the room and slamming the door.

It was not Frank I saw.
The darker thought that came to mind
was that it was the boy, years from now,
failed by me, abandoned
by what should have been.
The third more sobering thought – a rendering
of my own self in the not so distant future,
forsaken to my own strangeness,
unhealed and too far gone.

She said she didnt feel like going outside
to pee in the rain, and where
was a good bucket
for the middle of the night?
I told her it was in there, in the boy's room,
in Frank's old bedroom.
She went in and got the bucket.

I dug out a half flask of white Lambs
from under the floorboard behind the stove,
rigged up the propane burner

and slammed it back, hot, no sugar.
One more would have killed me, I'm sure,
and I wanted that one bad.

That night came the Hag.
She jammed a dead mouse down my throat
and I woke up choking the scream back
until a deep goatish bleat
burst from some dark crevice in me
and spooked me to my senses, for a time.

Later still I had to get my gal to walk
down the hall with me
to the makeshift latrine.
She helped me pull my one-piece down,
and set a spare bucket in front of me
to heave up in.
There was blood from both ends,
me reaching out for her at the edge
of candlelight: she was not there.
No idea how much time passed,
just cold and afraid to move
and afraid to suggest
that I couldnt walk past the doorway
of the very back room
on my own.

I started to bawl, for myself most likely,
or maybe so she might hear
and come mothering down the hall,
smelling like she does,
to help me up and clean me off,
suck all the venom out,
send me to sleep with a stroke and a song.

I sobbed and snotted as loud as I could until
I was certain, until I *knew*
that there was no room out there beyond
the peeling door,
that the house was gone,
no walls, no ceiling above,
only the tar-black Newfoundland night
and no God above watching over,
nothing but blood from both ends
and the tip of a dead mouse's tail in my throat.

Pay Off

Busted piston rod, my mechanic tells me.
Have to rebuild. Cost you more
than the bike is worth.
Give up on these two-strokes,
good for nostalgia and looks.
The rest is fuckin trouble.

I crunch my debts, grit my teeth against
the end of the month,
think again about hocking the guitar,
tug my eyebrows, punch a hole
in the new plaster,
finally put in a call
to the man himself
for a thousand dollars
to get me through motorcycle season.

He's mid-life now, gone vegan,
has emerged a handsome man
after all this absence, fit once more
to enjoy a little 250 cruiser
he splurged on last fall.

More than thirty years
since his own motorcycle days;
1973 Kawasaki 350
that suffered him through engineering
(a beast for speed, last of its kind,
rotting beyond restoration,
seized and dormant
in the damp grey basement
of the house he built
with his own two hands).

Nights I spent, wrecked on bad weed,
propped up on that bike,
revving the drowsy throttle
and probing for the young buck
he must have been.

One gravelly memory of his last ride:
nasal chainsaw echo burning up a cloud of dust
at the end of the Point Road before
the engine finally gave up the ghost.
Busted piston rod, no doubt,
if the fates do mock so openly.

Today, when I call, he answers.
So many years I want to cram into
this extravagant request,
but he agrees to the sum wholeheartedly
before I can even formulate the question.

An hour later he arrives outside my house
shaking his head
at the handwritten For Sale sign
I've taped to the handlebars,
at the loss of my beautiful
black and chrome two-stroke.
He doesnt have time for a cup of tea,
but he's brought twenty bills.

For a moment both of our hands
on the envelope, so that an outsider
would be hard pressed to fathom
who is the giver
and who is the taker.
And for an insider, given to suggestion,
I guess it's even harder to discern.

Something to Write Home About

Scrounging for days
for something to write home about,
but it's lazy up here on the hill
this time of year.

Everyone's out jamming leisure
down each other's throats,
rummaging, hunting
anxiously
for a place to settle in.

The shriek of the chainsaw still rips through my skull
and one mutant motherfucker of a blood-hungry nipper
would not let up
until my right eye was swollen shut.

The woman at the shop tells me
old Frank use to have the crows
eating out of his hand.
She stood on the step to smell my cigarette
and watch the cars blow past to Carbonear.

A little girl
leaning on the fence in the south meadow
who watches my kitchen window like a hawk:
a recurring dream.

That's all, for now.

TV Land tracked me down.
They want me to try a Wexford accent,
to come off scruffy

and scrappy and down on my luck.
I'll think hard about that one.

The theatre crowd called too,
to see if I wouldnt mind, terribly,
rewriting the whole second half
to make it more coherent, and to say
that the sex bits come off
just a tad gratuitous.
I dont know, I dont know,
about this opening night racket.

I have a belly full of trout sandwiches
and a broken toe, plenty of tobacco,
a desk full of rejected manuscripts,
all the engines are behaving as they should,
and Christ is it ever coming down out there,

hard enough to con me
into believing
that I'm onto something good.

The Way It Falls from the Sky

What else to do after they found me bleeding on the
waterfront that time? I holed up with a solid woman,
tapped my way through about a hundred-twenty
thousand words and forced them all on anyone foolish
enough to make eye contact. Signed some papers, got
a few phone calls and two years later I was strolling up
Queen West when I spotted a life-sized shot of myself
gawking out the window of a *bookshop* looking like some
born-again dope fiend gritting his teeth towards the
moment when a real human might finally catch on and
dim the fuckin lights a bit.

It's like that, sometimes. People want to shake your hand
and share their Demerol and say *well done yourself, you
gotta meet my girlfriend's sister,* and laugh about how much
you remind them of their brother out west or their
cousin in the Pen or some guy who once beat a horse
to death, and next they're burning you in effigy for this
thing that went down outside Nautical Nellie's one night
you weren't even in the country.

There you are, balanced on the jolly edge of a fifteen
hundred dollar *luncheon,* trying to tone down your
accent for the stuffed suit-and-tie dummies who have
such high hopes for that strange idea you mentioned,
and next you're dragging your bloody knuckles across
the graveyard wall on Duckworth at four oclock on a
Tuesday morning with the cops shaking you down for
identification and all they find in your pocket is a half
bottle of your mother's sleeping pills, a broken cigarette
and a one month sobriety chip.

Here you are, surveying the free goodies in some crushed velvet swag room on the eighteenth floor, loading up on designer colognes, and a month down the road she's padlocking you into the shower and conspiring with your ex to get you into some sort of program.

You find yourself haggling with the bank, holding hands with strangers, flossing and shaving, swinging blind at the deadlines, kicking at the undercarriage of your truck, almost calling your goddamn father, pining for the days when all anyone expected of you was to bleed out on the pissy waterfront, when the best you could muster was just under four hundred words and eye contact was of no concern at all.

Residents of the Lower Floors

One table left in the Dulcinea Room, in the back.
Bustling hump-day afternoon with the waiters
and cook staff roaring at each other in manic broken Spanish.
I flash my room key and a bottle of house red appears.
I've arrived somewhere.

Halfways through the bottle I'm bullshitting
about land and blue glass bottles
and sea rats and how to spot
where a moose hunkered down
and I feel her foot slip onto
the seat of my chair, her bare toes nudging me there.
I'm running out of time.

She asks who the hell was Dulcinea?
I slur on about the crazy old knight errant,
lippy Sancho and stubborn Rocinante.

We make hyper plans for her to cross the border with me
and bear my children.
The bill comes and I tell them
to add it to my room,
but as it happens, that privilege is not reserved
for residents of the lower floors.

Of course my credit card fails
and I've left my cash in the room upstairs.
She covers it with her company card,
but doesnt find it
quite as comical as I do.

Out on the street she abruptly remembers

a prior engagement.
I lean in to kiss her, but her lips are tight,
she wont meet my eye.
I need to know what's wrong, what's happened,
but she slips into a yellow cab and shouts instructions
for me to leave her cosmetics in a bag at the front desk.

For a good half hour
I stand on the curb, slack-jawed and stupid
until a man with sores leaking yellow
asks me for a cigarette
and I feel very far from home.
I've barely thought about my boy
for three days.

Scramble to the payphone in the restaurant lobby,
heaviness in my sinuses,
pulsing ache in my throat.
It's a busy signal, then an answering machine
then a low distant crackle.
Feel a sob rising up as I slam the receiver down
and wallop my forehead off the plaster
like any old bummed out movie cliché.

Some big bullfighting type from the kitchen
points a cheese grater at me, shouting *You go! You go!*

From over my shoulder, Senor Don Quixote, so-called madman,
stands snickering, pointing, rattling raspy laughter
from within crazed nooks
of his rust-battered armour,
justified yet again in what he's howled for centuries
about girls like his Dulcinea:
how they've ceased to exist,

how they never did exist,
how they exist exclusively
for the disenchantment of your heart.
Her sole earthly purpose?
To help you rise up to something
greater than you were designed to achieve.
And then to break you.

Back in the room, the sock she lost
that vanished beneath the bedclothes,
swallowed up in a bubble of lust,
suddenly resurfaces, folded smartly
on the edge of the bathtub.
Our toothbrushes crossed like lances
on the grudging lip of the sink,
and I cannot brush my teeth for days
for fear of furthering our estrangement.

I've Made An Arrangement

You always disappear, she says.
Where do you make off to?
You're strange like that.
Just when I think it's safe to settle
into a drink, I turn and you're not there.
Is it me? Is it me?
I'm trying not to take it personal.
I'm trying.

Now I know you dont like presents
but I do,
so you'll have to indulge me.

I saw you with what's-her-face
outside the women's toilet there.
Just, I dont know,
the way you were talking
and the look on your face.
And I know I'm not always around, see.
I suppose it has nothing to do with me,
ultimately.

So, go down and pick out
whichever one you fancy.
Just keep it under two hundred.
I've made an arrangement.
Well that's just it,
I want you to have a new one,
from me, but we both know
you'd never make it to the parlour
if I just *gave* you the cash.

I've heard a thing or two about that slut, by the way.
You might think she's all that, but you'll have to ask
some hard questions at some point.

You know I'd like that, yeah,
if you got something softer,
something with a bit of colour,
something maybe that made you
think of me.
But it's your body, your skin,
you'll have to live with it
for the rest of your life.

Anyhow, you know where to find me
when you get it all
out of your system.

Two Months

Got back two months later, a little past midnight, sinister
September chill hovering about the crusty doorstep, the
house scalding hot, reeking of stale absence and so sterile-
tidy I'm tempted to take my boots off. Flip through the mail
for any sign of a cheque. A barren letter from Ms. Noftall
to say her position's been shuffled, but to offer her sincere
respects for all my attempts at mending this past year. A
Chick-a-Dee subscription form with a special offer that ended
two months ago.

Surprised to find that I still have a phone number, I check
the messages: Alicia from Harlem to say she misses me,
worried, concerned, had a dream about me, that I was taking
her somewhere in her old boyfriend's Blazer, that I kept
nodding off at the wheel and laughing when she screamed
me awake. She says some things have opened up, some
folded in, some disappeared and there's not a soul, not a soul
out there in the sharp Manhattan night, and to please call as
soon as I get in.

Jon from Colonial, to say he saw my sister sitting in her red
car across the street from his house, pounding the pink fuzzy
steering wheel and crying her eyes out. He says he knocked
on her window to tell her that he was a friend of mine, that
if she needed anything, a place to lay low, cup of tea, not
to hesitate, not to think twice. He says he doesnt know the
situation, but anyways, he says, how are you? I hear maybe
you might be away for a while.

Tiana from Mississauga, to say my payment is past due and
my coverage will be terminated by a date come and gone
two months ago. Twelve messages to go and I erase them

all without listening. Wander about the property like an old graveyard ghost, jet-lagged and hollow, sweating out the free festival booze, while the downtown belches up at me with the bluster of some cornered creature that would sooner chew off its own balls than actually scrap it out.

Smoke my gums and tongue dry, listen to the neighbour's hushed fucking, lay my head down on a sullied feather pillow, gag on that thick swan stench, slide one of Amis's books off the shelf, flip a page, flip a page, absorbing nothing.

Another Night in Scilly Cove

Be nice to cut the shit tonight, break through somehow
– but the melody is barely audible across an impossible
span. Like to scrap all this tonight, but the dread sits chill,
unyielding, like a lately redundant mooring post that's
witnessed too many daybreak confessions and short-lived
loyalties.

There's a phone call that should have been made three
months ago, a fevered letter home scrawled on lurid hotel
stationery, sealed in a yellowing envelope and stashed in one
of the numerous junk drawers in the very back room.

Would have thought the hobbling days were come and gone.
But there are so many lost names, amends never to be made.

If I could ease these sullied lungs, settle the rush of blood in
this hard, thick skull, I could hear the ice in Desmond's glass
dissolving on the softer side of Trinity Bay.

Way Off Broadway

The boy is in Manhattan tonight.
Fancy that, my little man
holed up with his mama in a swank hotel.
Before he took to the skies he wanted to know
why they call it the Big Apple,
and didnt look too surprised I didnt know.

I am not in Manhattan tonight.
I'm *way* off Broadway, you might say.

In my more stranded moments
I picture him dashing out,
yellow cabs a rabid pack.
Or turning a busy corner
with trench-coated strangers,
never to be seen again.
More likely he's clinging to his mama's coattail,
munching on a famous hotdog.
Every fuckin thing is famous there –
lady with the torch,
Times Square flash and glory,
big cavity where the towers came down,
this café,
this newsstand,
this pothole.

Been trying my patience
by the greasy kerosene glow.
My head is a blur
of stubborn kings
and rubbish recollections,
of what went wrong with his mama and me:

If only I'd gone that way, that time,
instead of down there.

Fresh pencil, notebook, tea in the pot.
All the fixings if I was so inclined.
I dont miss the dog.
I dont miss the woman.

Outside, scrape some horse shit from my heel
and I'm struck briefly dumb by my own irrelevance.
The dogberry sludge, one shrivelled apple
clinging to the leeside tree,
the harbour swell, dishcloth on the line, the wood horse,
the oil drum. I dont miss the woman.
I dont miss the dog.

Back inside, I cram a grimy towel
in the gap beneath the porch door. Heave another junk
into the stove. Choke out the candles in the very back room.
Dash into the boy's room and out again.
Whisper something foolish in the horrible dark.

Acknowledgements

Special Thanks – for compassion, lenience, literary support, alliance, roast pheasant, funding, guidance, fancy teacups, gratuitous affection, belief, beds, acting gigs, renovations, foolish stories, invites and empty threats…

Percy Thomas and Sherry-Lynn. Shawn Bradley. Lois Brown. Creative Book Publishing. Michael Crummey. Mary Dalton. Paddy Daly. Beth Follett. Jason Fost. Alison Gzowski. Michelle Butler-Hallett. Harper Collins Canada. Blair Harvey. Ken Harvey. Dermot Healy. Krissy Holmes. Aislinn Hunter. Ron Hynes. Jerome Kennedy. Ruth Lawrence. NIFCO. NLAC. Marnie Parsons. Paula Pittman. Kristine Power. Resource Centre for the Arts. Jennice Ripley. Bob and Audrey and Jackie Rockett. Don Sedgwick. Suzanne Sicchia. Justin Simms. Sheila Sullivan. Todd Wall. Des Walsh. Perry Zimel. Gary and Dolores.

Joel Thomas Hynes is the celebrated author of the novels *Down to the Dirt* and *Right Away Monday*, and the acclaimed stage plays *The Devil You Dont Know, Say Nothing Saw Wood, Broken Accidents* and *Incinerator Road* (for young adults).

Recent awards include the 2008 NLAC Artist of the Year Award, the 2009 Lawrence Jackson Creative Writing Award, The 2009 Contra-Guys Award and the 2010 Cuffer Prize.

Also a professional actor, Hynes has performed numerous leading roles for stage, television and film, and recently wrote and directed his first film, *Clipper Gold*.